GIFTED
&
TALENTED®

*To develop
your child's gifts
and talents*

READING
BOOK TWO

A Workbook for Ages 6–8

Written by S. J. Williams
Illustrated by Larry Nolte

LOWELL HOUSE JUVENILE

LOS ANGELES

NTC/Contemporary Publishing Group

To Bruce, for his ebullience.
—S.J.W.

Published by Lowell House
A division of NTC/Contemporary Publishing Group, Inc.
4255 West Touhy Avenue, Lincolnwood (Chicago), Illinois 60646-1975 U.S.A.

Managing Director and Publisher: Jack Artenstein
Director of Publishing Services: Rena Copperman
Editorial Director, Juvenile: Brenda Pope-Ostrow
Director of Art Production: Bret Perry
Educational Editor: Linda Gorman
Typesetter: Carolyn Wendt

Lowell House books can be purchased at special discounts when ordered in bulk
for premiums and special sales. Please contact Customer Service at:
NTC/Contemporary Publishing Group
4255 W. Touhy Avenue
Lincolnwood, IL 60646-1975
1-800-323-4900

Printed and bound in the United States of America

ISBN: 1-56565-664-4

10 9 8 7 6 5 4 3 2 1

GIFTED & TALENTED® WORKBOOKS will help develop your child's natural talents and gifts by providing activities to enhance critical and creative thinking skills. These skills of logic and reasoning teach children **how to think**. They are precisely the skills emphasized by teachers of gifted and talented children.

Thinking skills are the skills needed to be able to learn anything at any time. Unlike events, words, and teaching methods, thinking skills never change. If a child has a grasp of how to think, school success and even success in life will become more assured. In addition, the child will become self-confident as he or she approaches new tasks with the ability to think them through and discover solutions.

GIFTED & TALENTED® WORKBOOKS present these skills in a unique way, combining the basic subject areas of reading, language arts, and math with thinking skills. The top of each page is labeled to indicate the specific thinking skill developed. Here are some of the skills you will find:

- Deduction—the ability to reach a logical conclusion by interpreting clues

- Understanding Relationships—the ability to recognize how objects, shapes, and words are similar or dissimilar; to classify or categorize

- Sequencing—the ability to organize events, numbers; to recognize patterns

- Inference—the ability to reach a logical conclusion from given or assumed evidence

- Creative Thinking—the ability to generate unique ideas; to compare and contrast the same elements in different situations; to present imaginative solutions to problems

Each book contains activities that challenge children. The activities range from easier to more difficult. You may need to work with your child on many of the pages, especially with the child who is a non-reader. However, even a non-reader can master thinking skills, and the sooner your child learns how to think, the better. Read the directions to your child and, if necessary, explain them. Let your child choose to do the activities that interest him or her. When interest wanes, stop. A page or two at a time may be enough, as the child should have fun while learning.

It is important to remember that these activities are designed to teach your child **how to think**, not how to find the right answer. Teachers of gifted children are never surprised when a child discovers a new "right" answer. For example, a child may be asked to choose the object that doesn't belong in this group: a table, a chair, a book, a desk. The best answer is **book**, since all the others are furniture. But a child could respond that all of them belong because they all could be found in an office or a library. The best way to react to this type of response is to praise the child and gently point out that there is another answer, too. While creativity should be encouraged, your child must look for the best and most **suitable** answer.

GIFTED & TALENTED® WORKBOOKS have been written and endorsed by educators. These books will benefit any child who demonstrates curiosity, imagination, a sense of fun and wonder about the world, and a desire to learn. They will open your child's mind to new experiences and help fulfill his or her true potential.

Read the sentences below. Then write each girl's name below her picture.

Naomi is going to play a game involving a hoop.

Tammy is going to play a game involving bases.

Maria is going to get wet.

_____   _____   _____

Read the story below. Then circle the picture that best fits the story.

Gretchen works in an optometrist's office. An optometrist is a doctor who tests people's eyesight and supplies glasses. Gretchen helps people pick out glasses that look good on them. Gretchen likes her work.

Roko, Bruce, and Alvin are entering a dogsled race. Each boy chose the dogs he wants to have on his dogsled team. Roko only chose dogs with a black spot over one eye. Bruce only chose dogs with big ears. Alvin only chose dogs with short tails.

On the line below each dog, write the name of the boy who chose it.

_____   _____   _____

_____   _____   _____

Jackie's kitten Cleo is missing. Can you find her? Read the clues below and draw a circle around Cleo.

Cleo does not have patches.
Cleo is not the largest cat.
Cleo has stripes on her back.
Cleo does not have stripes on her tail.

This is a photo of the Downey family. Today, someone in the Downey family is having a birthday. Can you figure out whose birthday it is? Read the clues below, then draw a circle around the birthday person.

The birthday person:
- is not wearing a tie.
- does not have a ponytail.
- is not the shortest person.
- is on the left side of the picture.

Read each group of words below. Circle the word in each group that could be used to describe the other words.

daisies
violets
flowers
roses
petunias

guitar
flute
drums
instrument
piano

Christmas
holiday
Easter
Thanksgiving
Hanukkah

ballet
tap
jazz
ballroom
dance

hike
crawl
run
move
walk

scared
feelings
sad
happy
excited

Draw a line from each group of words on the left to the word on the right that could go at the end of each word in the group.

| grocery
shoe
book | | bed |

| star
gold
sail | | light |

| flower
bunk
double | | room |

| flash
sun
moon | | fish |

| bath
living
bed | | store |

Read the story below, then circle the travel brochure that describes the place where Joseph should go.

Joseph wants to go somewhere that is hot. He enjoys sea kayaking. He likes to visit places where the people speak a language other than English.

COME SKI WITH US!

KAYAK THE CALIFORNIA COASTLINE

MEXICO AWAITS YOU

SEE THE FABULOUS FISH ON THE GREAT BARRIER REEF OF AUSTRALIA!

Read each sentence below. Cross out the word that doesn't belong. On the blank line, write a new word that will make the sentence make sense.

Karen slid on her slippers and stepped outside into the snow.

_____

Leroy's new pet goldfish chewed all the shoes in the house.

_____

The musician gently strummed her flute. _____

Jerry had a toothache so he went to see his barber. _____

Monika likes to swim in the lake because she loves the smell of salt water. _____

Harvey took his paintbrush and wrote a scary story.

_____

Frankie the spy is always in disguise. Read the clues to find Frankie. Draw a circle around him.

Frankie carries a cane.
Frankie always wears a hat.
Frankie has a mustache.
Frankie wears glasses.

Read the story, then answer the questions below.

Mona the cat lives in the city with her owner. Mona likes to explore the alleys in her neighborhood. One day, Mona set out in search of some fish bones for lunch. She found a big supply behind a seafood restaurant. After her meal, Mona found a lovely spot in the sunshine and settled in for a long nap.

Where does Mona live? _____

What did Mona go looking for? _____

_____

What do you think the fish bones were in when Mona found them? _____

_____

What did Mona do after she had lunch? _____

_____

Read the story. Draw a picture in the box below that shows what the story is about.

Poncho is a small gray dog. One day, Poncho was playing with his ball in the yard. Suddenly, the ball took a big bounce and landed in the middle of some prickly bushes. Poncho was sad because he couldn't get his ball. He barked until his owner came to fetch the ball out of the bushes.

Read the story. Fill in each blank with a word from the box below. Make sure the story makes sense.

Benny the blue jay lived in a large _____ in the city park. Benny loved to take a _____ in the fountain every morning. One day, Benny spotted a large cat _____ around the birdbath. Benny felt _____. He decided he would take his bath _____.

swim	jogging	bath
happy	house	later
tree	prowling	confused
sooner	scared	yesterday

What animals can swim? Think of as many as you can and write their names in the ocean on this page and the next. Write the names of animals that live underwater in the underwater spaces. Write the names of animals that can swim but don't live underwater in the spaces near the surface of the water.

Now draw pictures of all the animals you named.

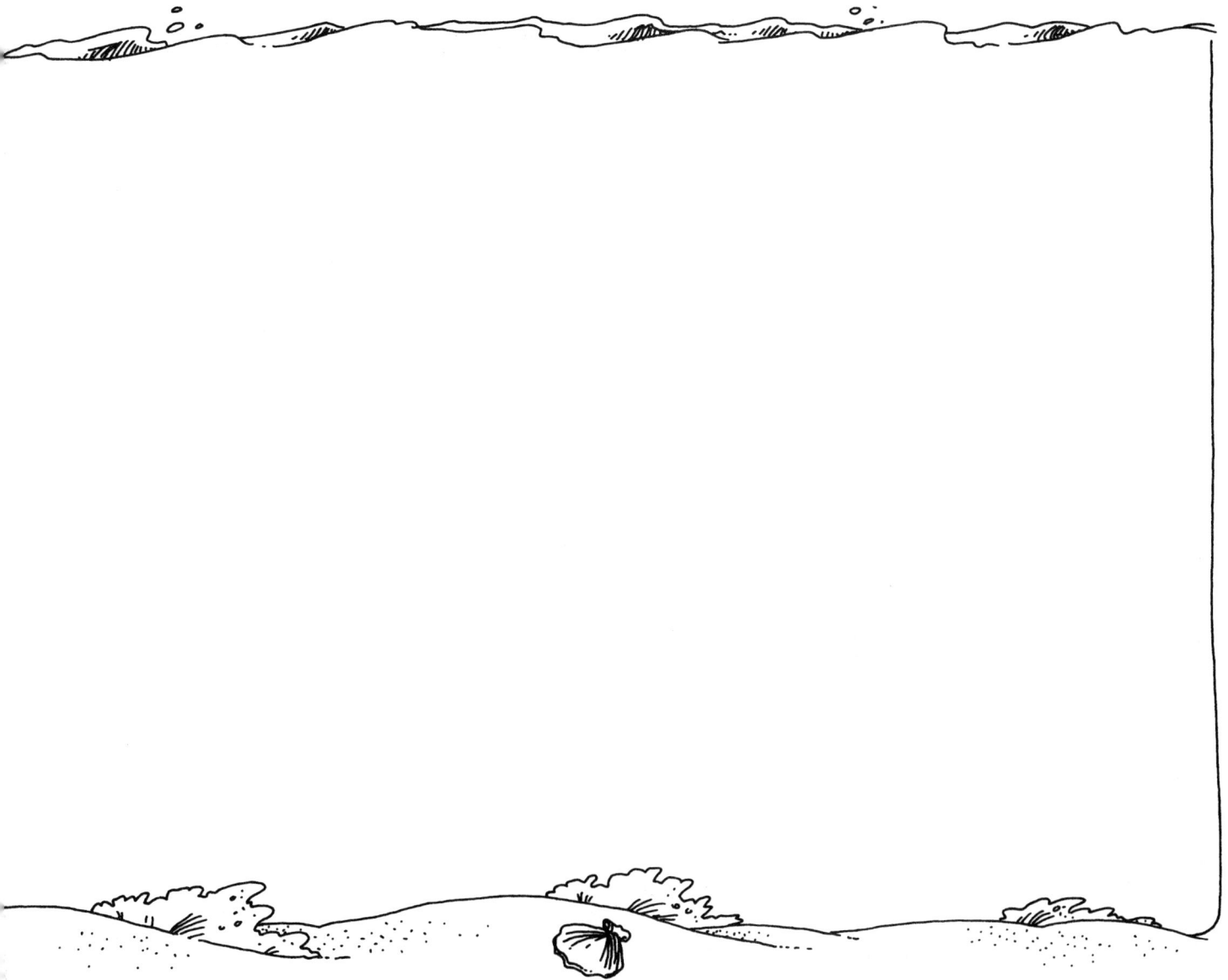

Read each pair of sentences. Fill in each blank line with a word that describes the words in **bold**.

Brian, Karl, and **David** each have a favorite hockey player.

The _____ each have a favorite hockey player.

Conan's farm has many **goats, pigs,** and **ducks**.

Conan's farm has many

_____.

Watching the **seagulls, terns,** and **sandpipers** on the beach mesmerized the cat.

Watching the _____ on the beach mesmerized the cat.

Geraldo used his telescope to see **Mars, Jupiter,** and **Saturn** in the night sky.

Geraldo used his telescope to see _____ in the night sky.

Read each pair of sentences. Fill in each blank line with a word that describes the words in **bold**.

Jennifer stood on the sand and listened to **the crashing of the waves, the cry of the birds,** and **the rush of the wind**.

Jennifer stood on the sand and listened to the _____ of the beach.

Ricky enjoys **surfing, sailing,** and **snorkeling**.

Ricky enjoys _____ sports.

Jason packed his **shirts, pants,** and **socks** for his trip to Colorado.

Jason packed his _____ for his trip to Colorado.

Cameron was lying in the field of **poppies, daisies,** and **lavender**.

Cameron was lying in the field of _____.

Simon and Susie like to play games. Simon's favorite games are played outdoors. He likes games that involve movement, like tag. He likes team games. Susie says that she has a new game for Simon to play.

What questions can Simon ask Susie to find out if he will like this new game?

1. _____

2. _____

3. _____

Mrs. Melody, the music teacher, is teaching her class a new song. The song is about a dragon and a boy who are friends and go camping in the mountains.

Which words below do you think might be in the song? Circle them.

fish	green	happy
ocean	fire	ride
run	ships	hike
tail	stars	tent
trees	train	marshmallows

For an extra challenge, make up a song about a dolphin and a girl who are friends. What are some of the words that you would use?

_____   _____   _____

_____   _____   _____

_____   _____   _____

The children in Mr. Wade's English class enjoy writing. Read the descriptions below that tell what each child likes to write about. Then look at the books on this page and the next and decide which child might have written each book. On each book cover, write the name of the author.

Dagmar enjoys writing about feelings.

Lorena loves to write about traveling.

Noel likes rivers.

Praveen is fascinated by dinosaurs.

Anita enjoys working with a hammer and nails.

Edith knows a lot about creatures in the ocean.

HOW TO BUILD A DOGHOUSE

by

_____

AROUND THE WORLD IN 8 MONTHS

by

_____

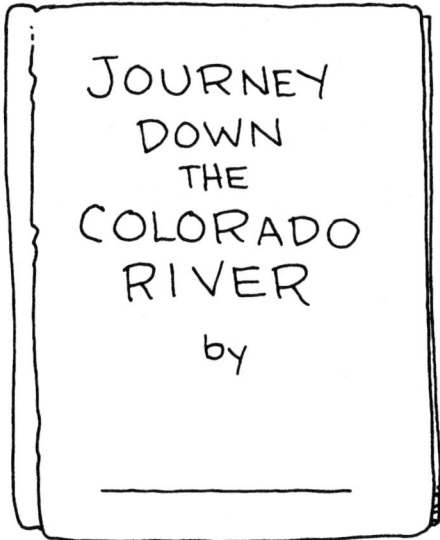

JOURNEY
DOWN
THE
COLORADO
RIVER

by

_____

HAPPY
OR SAD?
IT'S YOUR
CHOICE

by

_____

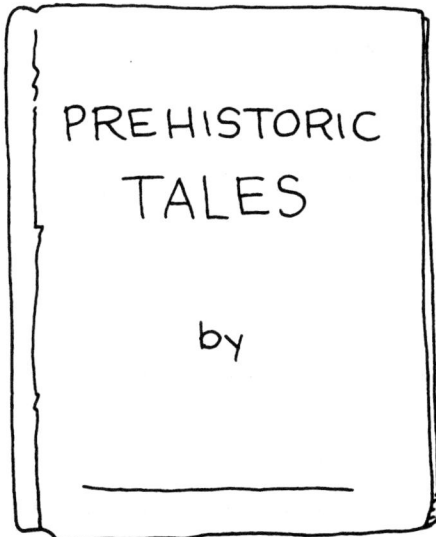

PREHISTORIC
TALES

by

_____

UNDERSEA
ADVENTURE

by

_____

Read the story, then answer the questions below.

Edward, the master barber of Suburbia, cut people's hair, dogs' hair, and trimmed bushes, too. As word spread around town, everyone was lining up with their dogs to get their hair cut. Soon, all the dogs in town had wild hairdos to match the haircuts of their owners! Edward had completely changed the face of Suburbia.

What effect did Edward have on the town of Suburbia?

_____

_____

What does the phrase **word spread** mean?

_____

Why do you think everyone wanted Edward to cut their hair?

_____

_____

Read the story, then answer the question below.

Mary Lou and Maggie love horses. At the Lucky Star Stables, they each have a favorite horse that they like to ride. Both of their horses have names that begin with **T** and end with a vowel.

Look at the horses and stalls below. On each door is the name of the horse that lives there. Which horses do Mary Lou and Maggie like to ride? Color those horses.

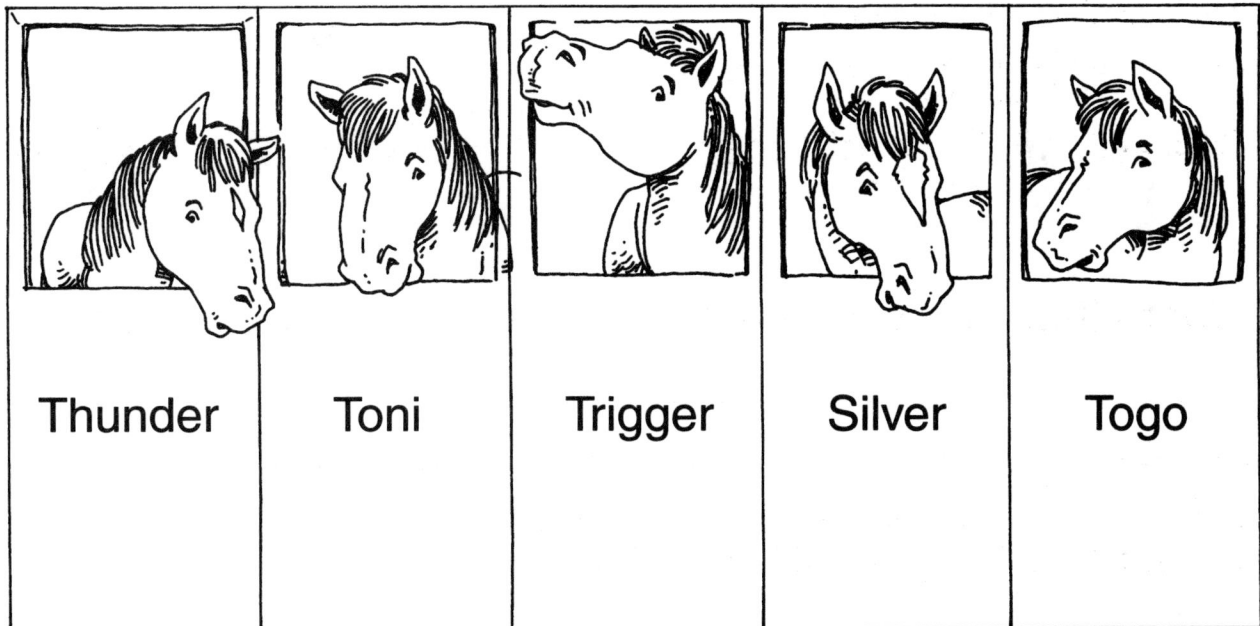

| Thunder | Toni | Trigger | Silver | Togo |

Read the story below. Then answer the questions on the next page.

Adam the ant lived happily underground with his ant family. Adam had always wanted to see what the world above ground looked like. His parents, however, forbade him from going above ground until he was older.

One night, after everyone had gone to sleep, Adam and his friends decided to see the world above ground for themselves. They came out of their ant hole and saw all the wonders of the world lit up by the moonlight. They saw tall pieces of grass and huge pebbles. Everything was so big! They crawled through an old sneaker and the holes of a rusty cheese grater. Then, suddenly, they met a hungry mouse searching for food. To them, it looked like a giant! Adam and his friends became very scared and fled back to their ant hole. They decided their parents were right to keep them underground until they were older.

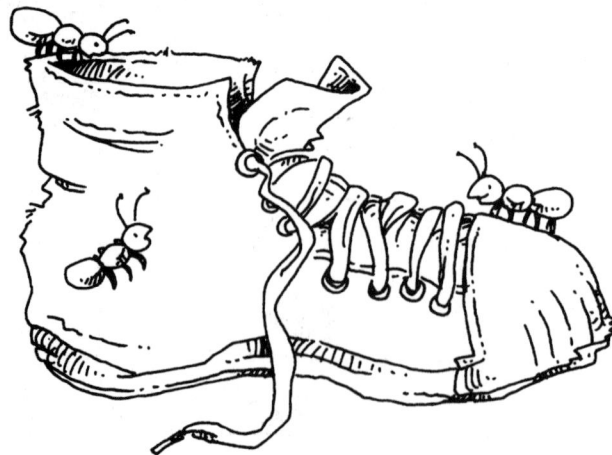

When did Adam and his friends go above ground?

_____

How were they able to see in the dark? _____

_____

What did they see first? _____

_____

Why did they get scared? _____

_____

How did they feel when they got home? _____

_____

Shannon and Ryan love amusement parks. Follow their path through the park. Then number the sentences below to mark the order in which they did things.

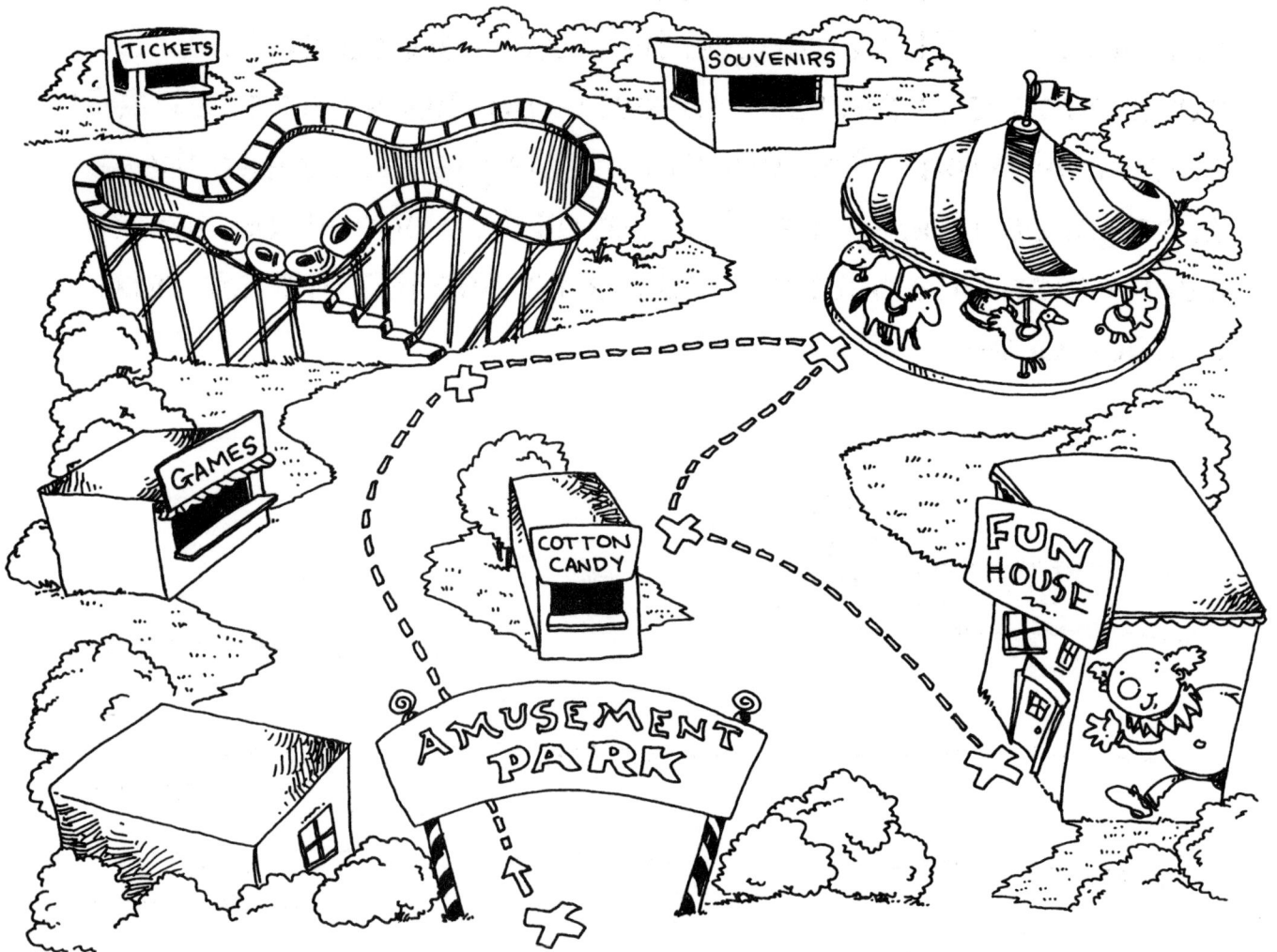

_____ They went through the Fun House.

_____ They rode on the roller coaster.

_____ They bought cotton candy.

_____ They rode on the carousel.

Read the story. Then label each row of plants below according to the facts of the story.

Renata spent the morning planting seeds in her garden. She planted roses, tomatoes, zucchini, eggplant, and strawberries. She arranged her rows very carefully. She put the roses in the row closest to her house so she could enjoy their smell. She put the purple plant between the zucchini and the roses. She put all the vegetables next to each other. She put the food plants with red in them next to each other.

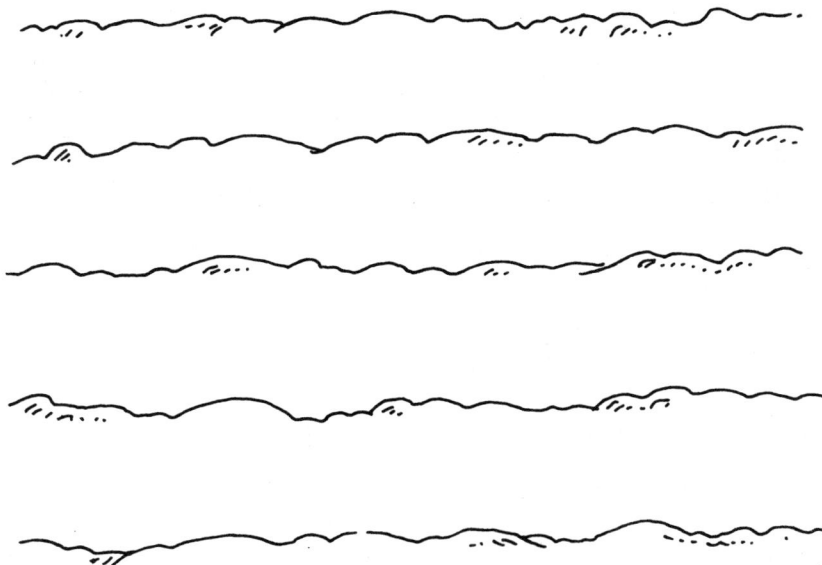

Read the story, then follow the directions below.

Many people do not like it when it rains. The rain forces them to stay indoors, where they get restless. But some things like it when it rains. Worms like rain because it loosens the dirt and allows them to crawl around the earth more freely. Worms don't like it when it's too sunny and dry!

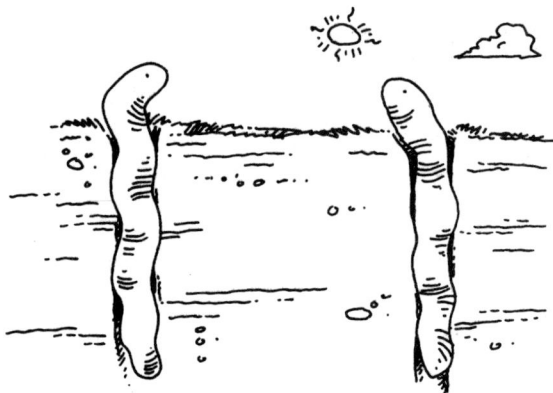

Think of something else that one group likes and another group dislikes. Write about it in the space below. Which group are you in?

_____

_____

_____

_____

_____

_____

Read the story, then follow the directions below.

Once there was a girl named Pamela who would not get out of her pajamas. She wore them night and day. Her pajama top had lots of stars on it and the bottoms had polka dots. Her pajama bottoms also had a hole in one knee.

Find Pamela's pajamas in the tops and bottoms below. Color her pajama top yellow. Color the bottoms blue.

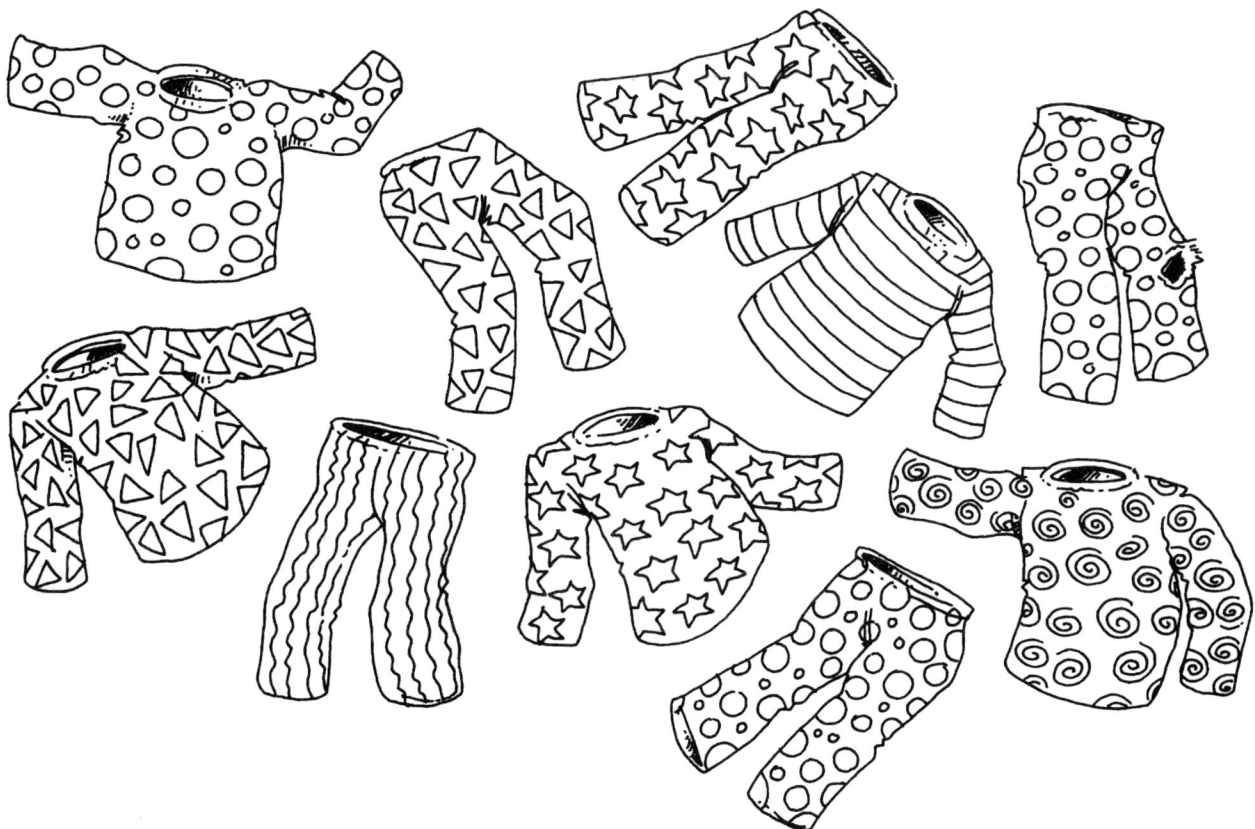

Read the story, then answer the questions below.

One day, James and his dog Chip went looking for Fluffy, a lost sheep. They tramped across a large field until they came upon a big hole. The hole was very dark. James was sure he heard voices coming from it. Shaking, he and Chip crept closer to the edge of the hole. Suddenly, Chip gave a yelp. James looked and saw a huge black shadow at the bottom of the hole. "Baaaa," said the shadow. It was Fluffy the sheep!

What were James and Chip looking for in the field?

_____

Was there any light in the hole?

_____

How do you think James felt as he looked down the hole?

_____

Did James and Chip find what they were looking for?

_____

Read the story. Then draw a picture in the box below that shows a scene in the story.

Annie was not like other children. Every night, she couldn't wait to go to bed. After she turned out the lights and got into bed, Annie would wake up the little people who had been sleeping under her covers all day. Annie and her little friends under the covers would laugh and play games. Annie's favorite friend under the covers was a two-inch tall woman named Mrs. Catelli. Mrs. Catelli told Annie the best stories she'd ever heard. If Annie ever felt sad, Mrs. Catelli could always cheer her up.

Read the story. Then color the picture below according to the facts in the story.

One corner of Miss Perry's classroom was designed for reading. The corner had lots of pillows on the floor so that her students could be comfortable while they read. Barbara's favorite pillow was the square purple pillow. She also liked the round green pillows and the triangle-shaped yellow pillows. The corner also had five blue pillows in the shapes of letters.

For an extra challenge, make as many words as you can using the letter pillows. Write the words on a separate piece of paper.

Read the story, then follow the directions below.

The children in Gillville love to fish. One cold Saturday, they bundled up in warm clothes and went to the dock to see what they could catch. Manny wore a striped scarf and caught the longest fish. Sven caught the smallest fish and wore a furry hat. Gabriel caught a striped fish and wore thick gloves. Jeffrey wore his heaviest jacket and caught the heaviest fish.

Draw a line from each boy to the fish he caught.

Read the story below. Then follow the directions on the next page.

Kim loved to go out with his mother. On one especially busy day, they did five errands! First, they dropped off their bottles and cans at the recycling center. Next, they dropped off a pair of shoes at the shoe repair. Then they picked up some photos at the film developer. After that, they picked up some clothes at the dry cleaner. Then Kim waited while his mother donated blood at the blood donor center. Kim and his mother celebrated the end of their busy day by having ice-cream cones.

Draw a line through the town to show the order in which Kim and his mother did their errands.

For an extra challenge, can you think of a quicker way that Kim and his mother could have done their errands? On a separate piece of paper, write the errands in a faster order.

Read the story. Then finish it on the lines below.

Oscar the sea otter loved to play in the ocean on windy days. He would dive and frolic in the waves for hours. One day, Oscar was floating on his back with an abalone shell on his belly when he spotted a sea kayak in the distance. The person in the kayak paddled closer to Oscar to get a better look at him.

What happened next between Oscar and the person in the kayak? _____

_____

_____

_____

_____

_____

_____

_____

Analogies are statements that compare two things to each other. Read each sentence and decide how the first pair of words is related. Next, think of a word that completes the analogy by making the second pair of words relate in the same way as the first pair.

1. Dark is to night as
   light is to _____.

2. Flipper is to whale as
   arm is to _____.

3. Ice cream is to milk shake as
   flour is to _____.

4. Shiver is to cold as
   sweat is to _____.

5. Red is to apple as
   yellow is to _____.

6. Whisker is to kitten as
   beard is to _____.

Analogies are statements that compare two things to each other. Read each sentence and decide how the first pair of words is related. Next, think of a word that completes the analogy by making the second pair of words relate in the same way as the first pair.

1. Leap is to dance as
   step is to _____.

2. Bake is to oven as
   chill is to _____.

3. Frog is to green as
   polar bear is to _____.

4. Spotted is to leopard as
   striped is to _____.

5. Soap is to clean as
   mud is to _____.

6. Volcano is to lava as
   fountain is to _____.

Read each sentence and decide how the pair of words is alike. Write the word that describes how they are alike on the blank line.

1. The ocean and the sky are _____.

2. Carrots and celery are _____.

3. The Sun and bananas are _____.

4. Forks and spoons are _____.

5. Penguins and owls are _____.

6. Carousels and Ferris wheels are _____.

7. Trumpets and violins are _____.

8. Rocks and cement are _____.

Read each sentence and decide how the pair of words is alike. Write the word that describes how they are alike on the blank line.

1. Tigers and zebras are

   _____.

2. Round and square are

   _____.

3. Buses and cars are

   _____.

4. Winter and summer are

   _____.

5. Baseball and football are

   _____.

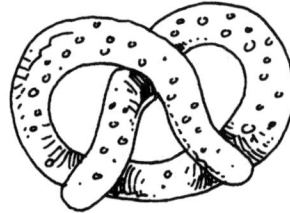

6. Pillows and cotton balls are

   _____.

7. Pretzels and chips are

   _____.

8. Honey and glue are

   _____.

A **fact** is something that is always true. An **opinion** is what someone thinks or feels. Decide whether each sentence states a fact or gives an opinion. If it states a fact, circle **F**. If it states an opinion, circle **O**.

1. Penguins can't fly.   F   O

2. Peacocks are beautiful birds.   F   O

3. There are seven days in a week.   F   O

4. Some children don't like broccoli.   F   O

5. Learning to play the piano is easy.   F   O

6. Earth is the third planet from the Sun.   F   O

7. Riding a roller coaster is fun.   F   O

8. Spiders are creepy.   F   O

  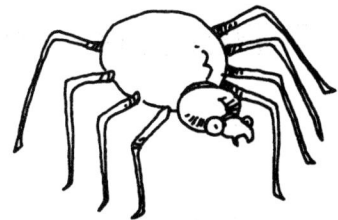

Analogies are statements that compare two things to each other. Read each sentence and decide how the first pair of words is related. Next, think of a word that completes the analogy by making the second pair of words relate in the same way as the first pair.

1. Whale is to ocean as moose is to _____.

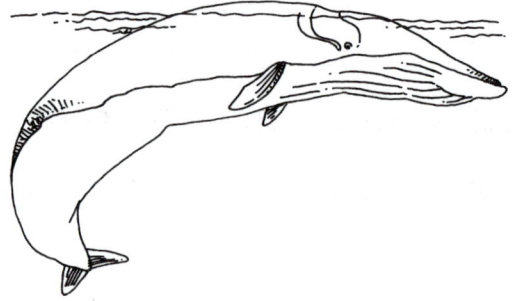

2. Boat is to lake as airplane is to _____.

3. Brush is to painting as needle is to _____.

4. Teeth are to mouth as seeds are to _____.

5. Scratch is to dull as polish is to _____.

6. Office is to working as tent is to _____.

Read the story, then answer the questions below.

Russell, Robin, and Aaron went to the beach one day. They put on sunblock and sat on their towels. Aaron stared out at the ocean. Suddenly, he shouted, "Look!" Russell and Robin immediately looked at the ocean, too.

Offshore, a huge whale's back broke the surface of the water. The whale exhaled a great burst of breath and spouted a beautiful spray of water.

Why did the boys put on sunblock? _____

_____

What did Aaron see in the ocean? _____

What did the whale do? _____

_____

How do you think the boys felt about seeing the whale?

_____

Read the story, then read the statements that follow. If the statement is true, circle **T**. If the statement is false, circle **F**.

Thomas teaches a yoga class every Saturday. He always wears red shorts and a white T-shirt. The class lasts one hour. The class is always full.

1. Thomas is a yoga teacher.   **T**   **F**

2. Thomas's class is held twice a week.   **T**   **F**

3. The class is 60 minutes long.   **T**   **F**

4. Not everyone enrolled in the class
   comes every week.   **T**   **F**

5. Thomas sometimes wears his favorite
   blue shorts in class.   **T**   **F**

Read the story. Add things to the picture below to make it match the story.

One beautiful, sunny day, Nicholas and Katherine rode their bicycles through the park. Both of them wore safety helmets. They saw a squirrel running up a tree and a rabbit chewing on some grass. Nicholas and Katherine had a great time in the park!

Look at each picture. Make up a title for each picture and write it on the line. Your title should tell what the picture is about in just a few words.

Title: _____

Title: _____

Look at each picture. Make up a title for each picture and write it on the line. Your title should tell what the picture is about in just a few words.

Title: _____

Title: _____

Read the story, then read each incomplete statement that follows. Decide which suggested word best completes the statement. Write that word on the blank line.

Michelle studies the way tortoises live in the desert. She is learning where they go when it is cold, what they eat, and how long they can go without water.

1. Michelle is a _____.   student   teacher

2. Tortoises live in the _____.   ocean   desert

3. Michelle is learning where tortoises go when it is _____.   cold   hot

4. Michelle is learning how long tortoises can go without _____.   food   water

Read the story, then read the statements that follow. If the statement is true, circle **T**. If the statement is false, circle **F**.

On Sunday, Gordon went to the zoo to see his favorite animals, the fruit bats. The zoo has a dozen fruit bats. The zookeeper told Gordon that fruit bats in the wild live mostly in Africa and Asia.

1. Fruit bats live only at the zoo.   T   F

2. Gordon had to miss school to go
   to the zoo.   T   F

3. Gordon's favorite animals at the zoo
   are fruit bats.   T   F

4. Fruit bats in the wild live mostly
   in South America.   T   F

5. There are 12 fruit bats at the zoo.   T   F

Who, what, where, when, why, and how are called **question words** because we use them when we ask questions.

Read the sentence. Answer each question word that follows by writing the part of the sentence that gives that information.

After taking a deep breath, Ray cautiously opened the closet door in the haunted house to see what was inside.

Who? _____

What? _____

Where? _____

When? _____

Why? _____

How? _____

How do you think Ray felt as he opened the door?

_____

_____

_____

Read the statements below. On each blank line, write a word that means the same as the word **said**. The first one is done for you.

1. "I'm too tired to hike the rest of the way," ___complained___ the boy.

2. "I'm so excited to ride the giant roller coaster!" _____ Rusty.

3. "Spot, get off the couch!" _____ Dorothy.

4. "Don't tell Grandma about her surprise party," _____ Paula.

5. "Ahhh! There's a spider in my room!" _____ Charlotte.

Each sentence below is the answer to a question. On the line above each sentence, write the question.

_____

Roses come in red, yellow, white, orange, pink, and purple.

_____

Dad will be home at five o'clock.

_____

The capital of the United States is Washington, D.C.

_____

Mother gray whales swim up the coast with their new calves in April and May every year.

WASHINGTON
D.C.

Each sentence below is the answer to a question. On the line above each sentence, write the question.

_____

The Statue of Liberty was given to the United States by France.

_____

Halloween is on October 31 every year.

_____

An elephant can live up to 65 years.

_____

Our hearts pump blood through our bodies.

Write a story about what is happening in the picture. What is each character in the picture doing? What do you think each character is thinking?

_____

_____

_____

_____

_____

_____

_____

_____

_____

_____

Look closely at the picture. When you think you can remember what is in the picture, turn the page.

Now circle only the items that you saw in the picture on the previous page.

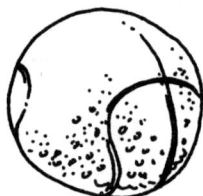

Answers

Page 5
From left to right, the girls are:
Tammy   Naomi   Maria

Page 6
Circle this picture:

Page 7

Alvin   Bruce   Roko

Roko   Alvin   Bruce

Page 8

Page 9

Page 10
Circle these words:
flowers   instrument
holiday   dance
move   feelings

Page 11
grocery, shoe, book: store
star, gold, sail: fish
flower, bunk, double: bed
flash, sun, moon: light
bath, living, bed: room

Page 12
Circle this brochure:

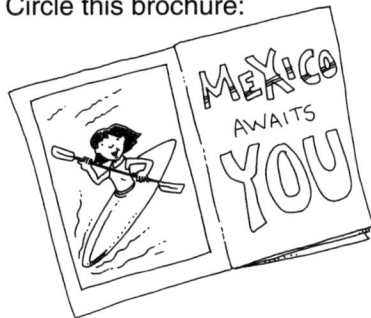

Page 13
Change *slippers* to *boots.*
Change *goldfish* to *puppy* or *dog.*
Change *flute* to *guitar, banjo,*
or *harp.*
Change *barber* to *dentist.*
Change *lake* to *ocean.*
Change *paintbrush* to *pencil*
or *pen.*

Page 14

Page 15
Sample answers:
Mona lives in the city.
She went looking for some fish
bones for lunch.
The fish bones were in a
garbage can.
She found a lovely spot in the
sunshine and settled in for a
long nap.

Page 16
Pictures will vary.
Parent: Make sure child's picture
illustrates a part of the story.

Page 17
tree
bath
prowling
scared
later

Pages 18–19
Answers and pictures will vary.
Some animals that live underwater
include fish, turtles, whales,
dolphins, sharks, and octopuses.
Some animals that can swim
but don't live underwater include
seals, penguins, sea otters,
and ducks.

Page 20
boys
animals
birds
planets

Page 21
sounds
water
clothes
flowers

Page 22
1. Is the game played outdoors?
2. Does the game involve
   movement?
3. Is the game played by teams?

Page 23

Answers will vary, though words likely to be in the song are:

trees	hike
fire	tent
stars	marshmallows
happy	

Extra challenge: Words will vary.

Pages 24–25

"How to Build a Doghouse" by Anita

"Around the World in 8 Months" by Lorena

"Journey Down the Colorado River" by Noel

"Happy or Sad? It's Your Choice" by Dagmar

"Prehistoric Tales" by Praveen

"Undersea Adventure" by Edith

Page 26

Sample answers:

Edward completely changed the way the people, dogs, and bushes looked in Suburbia.

Word spread means that information was passed along to more and more people. Everyone wanted Edward to cut their hair because he was a master barber who had talent and creativity.

Page 27

Color Toni and Togo.

Pages 28–29

Sample answers:

They went above ground one night after everyone had gone to sleep.

They were able to see because the moonlight lit everything up.

First they saw tall pieces of grass.

They got scared because the mouse they saw looked like a giant to them.

They were glad to be home. They decided that their parents were right to keep them underground until they were older.

Page 30

__4__ They went through the Fun House.

__1__ They rode on the roller coaster.

__3__ They bought cotton candy.

__2__ They rode on the carousel.

Page 31

From top to bottom, the rows should be:

roses
eggplant
zucchini
tomatoes
strawberries

Page 32

Answers will vary.

Page 33

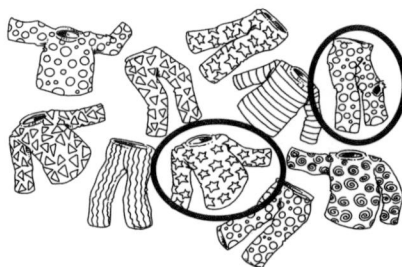

Parent: Make sure child colors circled top yellow and circled bottoms blue.

Page 34

Sample answers:

They were looking for Fluffy, a lost sheep.

No, the hole was very dark.

James felt scared because he didn't know what was in the hole.

Yes, they found Fluffy the sheep.

Page 35

Pictures will vary.

Parent: Make sure child's picture illustrates a part of the story.

Page 36

Parent: Make sure child colors the pillows in the picture as follows:

square pillow—purple
round pillows—green
triangle-shaped pillows—yellow
letter-shaped pillows—blue

Extra challenge: Some words that could be made from the letters include sat, rat, tar, tear, eat, ate, seat, star, stare, and rate.

Page 37

Pages 38–39

Draw a line through the town as follows:

- to the recycling center
- from the recycling center to the shoe repair
- from the shoe repair to the film developer
- from the film developer to the dry cleaner
- from the dry cleaner to the blood donor center
- from the blood donor center to the ice-cream shop

Extra challenge: A faster route would be recycling center, dry cleaner, shoe repair, ice-cream shop, film developer, and blood donor center.

Page 40

Answers will vary.

Page 41

1. day
2. person, human being
3. cake, bread
4. hot
5. banana, pear, lemon
6. man

Page 42

1. walk
2. refrigerator
3. white
4. tiger, zebra

5. dirty
6. water

Page 43
1. blue
2. vegetables
3. yellow
4. utensils
5. birds
6. round, rides
7. instruments
8. hard

Page 44
1. striped
2. shapes
3. vehicles
4. seasons
5. sports
6. soft
7. salty, snack foods
8. sticky

Page 45
1. F
2. O
3. F
4. F
5. O
6. F
7. O
8. O

Page 46
1. forest
2. sky
3. sewing
4. fruit, vegetable
5. shiny
6. camping

Page 47
Sample answers:
They put on sunblock to protect their skin from the Sun.
Aaron saw a whale's back breaking the surface of the water.
The whale exhaled a great burst of breath and spouted a beautiful spray of water.
The boys were very excited.

Page 48
1. T
2. F
3. T
4. F
5. F

Page 49
Parent: Make sure child adds the Sun in the sky, a helmet on the girl's head, a squirrel running up a tree, and a rabbit chewing on some grass.

Page 50
Titles will vary.

Page 51
Titles will vary.

Page 52
1. student
2. desert
3. cold
4. water

Page 53
1. F
2. F
3. T
4. F
5. T

Page 54
Who? Ray
What? opened the closet door
Where? in the haunted house
When? after taking a deep breath
Why? to see what was inside
How? cautiously
Sample answer: Ray felt scared as he opened the door.

Page 55
1. complained, moaned
2. shouted, cried
3. yelled, shouted
4. whispered
5. screamed, yelled, shouted

Page 56
Sample answers:
What colors do roses come in?

What time will Dad be home?
What is the capital of the United States?
When do mother whales swim up the coast with their new calves?

Page 57
Who gave the Statue of Liberty to the United States?
When is Halloween?
How long can an elephant live?
What do our hearts do?

Page 58
Stories will vary.

Pages 59–60

Other **GIFTED & TALENTED®**

books that will help develop your child's gifts and talents

Workbooks:
- Reading (4–6) $4.95
- Reading Book Two (4–6) $4.95
- Math (4–6) $4.95
- Math Book Two (4–6) $4.95
- Language Arts (4–6) $4.95
- Puzzles & Games for
  Reading and Math (4–6) $4.95
- Puzzles & Games for
  Reading and Math Book Two (4–6) $4.95
- Puzzles & Games for
  Critical and Creative Thinking (4–6) $4.95
- Phonics (4–6) $4.95
- Phonics Puzzles & Games (4–6) $4.95
- Math Puzzles & Games (4–6) $4.95
- Reading Puzzles & Games (4–6) $4.95
- Reading (6–8) $4.95
- Reading Book Two (6–8) $4.95
- Math (6–8) $4.95
- Math Book Two (6–8) $4.95
- Language Arts (6–8) $4.95
- Puzzles & Games for
  Reading and Math (6–8) $4.95
- Puzzles & Games for
  Reading and Math, Book Two (6–8) $3.95
- Puzzles & Games for
  Critical and Creative Thinking (6–8) $4.95
- Phonics (6–8) $4.95
- Phonics Puzzles & Games (6–8) $4.95
- Math Puzzles & Games (6–8) $4.95
- Reading Puzzles & Games (6–8) $4.95
- Reading Comprehension (6–8) $4.95

Reference Workbooks:
- Word Book (4–6) $4.95
- Almanac (6–8) $3.95
- Atlas (6–8) $3.95
- Dictionary (6–8) $3.95

Story Starters:
- My First Stories (6–8) $5.95
- Stories About Me (6–8) $5.95
- Stories About Animals (6–8) $4.95

Science Workbooks:
- The Human Body (4–6) $5.95
- Animals (4–6) $5.95
- The Earth (4–6) $5.95
- The Ocean (4–6) $5.95

Question & Answer Books:
- The Gifted & Talented® Question &
  Answer Book for Ages 4–6 $5.95
- Gifted & Talented® More Questions &
  Answers for Ages 4–6 $5.95
- Gifted & Talented® Still More
  Questions & Answers for
  Ages 4–6 $5.95
- The Gifted & Talented® Question &
  Answer Book for Ages 6–8 $5.95
- Gifted & Talented® More Questions &
  Answers for Ages 6–8 $5.95
- Gifted & Talented® Still More
  Questions & Answers for
  Ages 6–8 $5.95
- Gifted & Talented® Science Questions
  & Answers: The Human Body
  for Ages 6–8 $5.95

For Preschoolers:
- Alphabet Workbook $5.95
- Counting Workbook $5.95

Drawing:
- Learn to Draw (6 and up) $5.95

For Parents:
- How to Develop Your Child's Gifts
  and Talents During the Elementary
  Years $11.95
- How to Develop Your Child's Gifts and
  Talents in Math $15.00
- How to Develop Your Child's Gifts and
  Talents in Reading $15.00
- How to Develop Your Child's Gifts and
  Talents in Vocabulary $15.00
- How to Develop Your Child's Gifts and
  Talents in Writing $15.00

For orders, call 1-800-323-4900.